THE SCIENCE BEHIND

Homes

Chris Oxlade

Raintree

Chicago, Illinois

www.capstonepub.com
Visit our website to find out
more information about
Heinemann-Raintree books.

To order:
☎ Phone 888-454-2279
💻 Visit www.capstonepub.com
to browse our catalog and order online.

Edited by Claire Throp, Megan Cotugno,
    and Vaarunika Dharmapala
Designed by Steve Mead
Original illustrations © Capstone Global Library
    Ltd 2012
Illustrations by Oxford Designers & Illustrators
Picture research by Ruth Blair

Originated by Capstone Global Library Ltd
Printed and bound in China by Leo Paper
    Products Ltd

15 14 13 12 11
10 9 8 7 6 5 4 3 2 1

**Library of Congress Cataloging-in-Publication
Data**
Oxlade, Chris.
  Homes / Chris Oxlade.
      p. cm.—(The science behind)
  Includes bibliographical references and index.
  ISBN 978-1-4109-4488-7 (hc)—ISBN 978-1-4109-
4499-3 (pb) 1. Dwellings—Juvenile literature. 2.
Housing—Juvenile literature. I. Title.
  TH4811.5.O95 2012
  690'.8—dc23   2011014582

Acknowledgments
We would like to thank the following for
permission to reproduce photographs: Getty
Images p. **18** (Dimitri Vervitsiotis); Photolibrary
pp. **6** (Collection Leber), **19** (Tessa Bunney),
25 (JGI/Blend Images); Shutterstock pp. **5**
(© Nikonaft), **7** (© jaddingt), **8** (© Michael-John
Wolfe), **9** (© Christina Richards), **11** (© Dmitry
Naumov), **13** (© Mircea Maties), **16** (© Foto011),
20 (© Keith Bell), **20** (© kzww), **20** (© Terekhov
Igor), **22** (© Tomas Skopal), **23** (© Monkey
Business Images).

Cover photograph reproduced with permission
of Shutterstock (© Andy Z.).

We would like to thank Nancy Harris for her
invaluable help in the preparation of this book.

Contents

Look for these boxes:

Stay safe
These boxes tell you how to keep yourself and your friends safe from harm.

In your day
These boxes show you how science is a part of your daily life.

Measure up!
These boxes give you some fun facts and figures to think about.

Some words appear in bold, **like this**. You can find out what they mean by looking at the green bar at the bottom of the page or in the glossary.

Science in Your Home

What is a home?

A home is a place that gives you shelter and keeps you safe. It protects you from the cold, from hot sunshine, and from wind and rain. Inside is a space where you can play, sleep, cook, eat, and wash.

You might have lived in your home for a long time. You probably do not think about how your home keeps you warm, or why water comes out of the kitchen faucet, or about the materials it is made of.

You might not know it, but science is at work everywhere in your home. If you learn about this science, you can understand how your home works.

In your day

When you take milk out of the refrigerator, do you think about why the milk is cold? It is because of science. The refrigerator makes things cold by taking heat out of the space inside it. The heat comes out of the back of the refrigerator into the air.

These are just some of the parts of a house that use science to make them work.

roof tiles

drain

walls

electric lights

floor

Building Homes

Imagine taking the furniture, carpets, curtains, and all the other things out of your home. What would be left? The answer is walls, floors, and a roof. These parts make up the **structure** of your home.

In some homes, the walls are made up of materials such as stone, brick, or **concrete**. These are very strong materials. They hold up the floors and the roof. There are holes in the walls for windows and doors.

A house stays dry inside when it rains. This is because the roof is made from waterproof tiles. These will not let any water soak through.

structure   strong shape that holds up a building
concrete   very hard building material, similar to rock

Holding it up

Some homes have a **frame** made of wood, concrete, or a strong metal called steel. The frame holds up the floors, roof, and walls. Apartment buildings always have a frame. The frame rests on top of strong **foundations**. One job of the walls and the roof is to keep out rain and snow. They make a home waterproof.

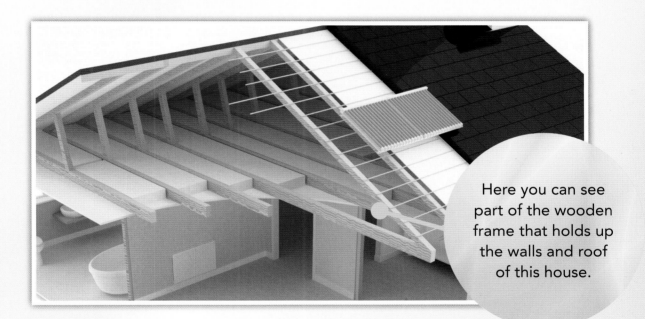

Here you can see part of the wooden frame that holds up the walls and roof of this house.

In your day

On your way to school or while running errands, look out for new homes being built. This is a good time to see the structure of a home. Look for frames, walls, floors, and roofs being made.

frame   pieces of concrete and metal joined together that hold up a building
foundation   part of a home that stops it from sinking into the ground

Do you know what materials your house is built from?

Building materials

Materials that are often used for building homes are wood, brick, stone, concrete, steel, glass, and plastic. Each of these materials has its own **properties**. The properties of a material include how strong it is, how easily it bends, how easy it is to cut, and its **texture**. Builders choose materials for building homes because of their properties.

property   what a material is like (such as how hard it is)
texture   how a material feels (whether it is rough or smooth)

Cement and concrete

Cement is a useful material for building homes. When it is mixed with water, it slowly becomes very hard. Cement mixed with sand and water makes **mortar**. Mortar is used to stick bricks together. Concrete is made by adding gravel to mortar.

In your day

You use materials every day. At school, you might make models with different materials, such as plastic bottles and cardboard. Think about why you choose these materials. Would you make a water container from cardboard? Why not?

This builder is spreading out concrete to make the floor of a house.

cement	gray powder that turns hard when it gets wet
mortar	solid material made from cement and sand

Keeping Warm and Keeping Cool

Central heating keeps homes warm. A central-heating system may have a **boiler**, where **fuel** such as gas is burned. When the fuel burns, it makes heat. The heat warms up water in the boiler. The water flows along pipes to radiators (heaters) around the house. Heat from the radiators goes into the rooms. Hot water cools in radiators and goes back to the boiler. A machine called a thermostat controls the home's **temperature**.

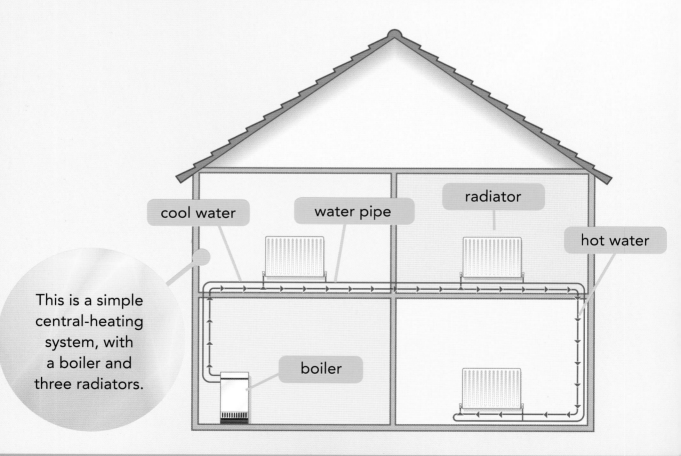

cool water

water pipe

radiator

hot water

This is a simple central-heating system, with a boiler and three radiators.

boiler

boiler machine that burns fuel to heat water
fuel material we burn to make heat or power, such as gas, oil, or coal

Forced-air heating

Many houses also have **forced-air heating**. Heat is created by oil, gas, or **electricity** in a central air handling unit. This unit has a powerful fan or blower. It sends the heated air through the house using air ducts (passageways) and vents (openings in rooms).

Here you can see burning gas heating up a boiler.

Stay safe

You must be careful if you are near radiators and other heaters. They could burn you if you touch them. Do not put towels or clothes on radiators, because the heat can make them catch fire.

temperature   how hot or cold something is
forced-air heating   heating system that spreads warm air through ducts and vents

Keeping heat in

When it is cold outside, heat leaks out of your home through the walls, the windows, and the roof. Heating is needed to replace the heat that escapes, and to keep your home warm. We stop heat from escaping by using **insulation**.

Modern windows have two sheets of glass with a space between them. This helps to stop heat from escaping through the glass. This type of window is called double-glazing.

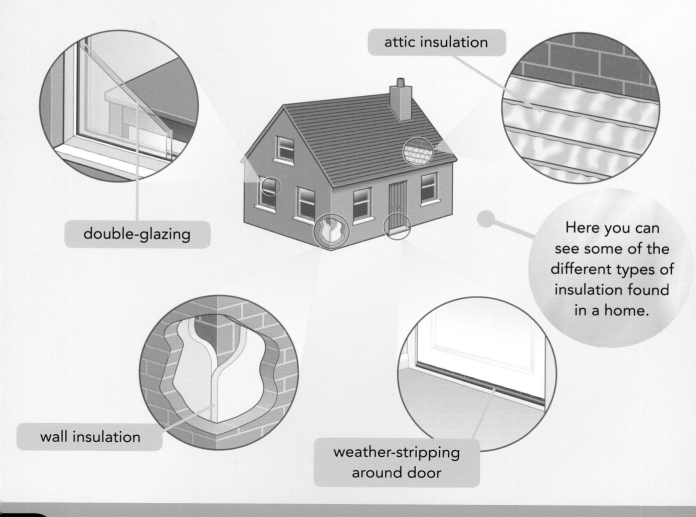

attic insulation

double-glazing

Here you can see some of the different types of insulation found in a home.

wall insulation

weather-stripping around door

insulation   material that stops heat from leaking out of a home

Keeping heat out

You might live in a place where the weather is often hot. In that case, you have to keep your home cool. Heat comes from sunshine. Shutters and shades over windows help to stop a home from heating up.

Shutters keep hot sunshine out. They keep a home cool.

In your day

Insulation in your home is hidden, but you can see insulation in other places. On a cold day, you wear layers of clothes. All those layers trap air and stop heat from escaping from your body. Home insulation works in the same way.

Electricity

How many things in your bedroom need **electricity** to work? Don't forget to count the lights! Your home is full of electric machines and electric lights. It has a supply of electricity. The electricity goes to each room along wires called cables. Cables are found in the walls and under the floors. Some electricity goes to wall **sockets**, and some goes to light bulbs.

Heat

Electricity can easily be turned into heat, movement, and light. When you plug a hair dryer into a wall socket and switch it on, electricity flows from the socket to the hair dryer. The hair dryer's motor spins, and this warms up its heating **elements**. This produces the heat that dries your hair.

Stay safe

The electricity that comes from wall sockets is very powerful. So is the electricity that lights up bulbs. Never poke anything into a wall socket or light socket. You could be badly injured.

electricity   form of energy used to make light and heat, and to power machines
socket   place where you can plug in an electric machine

Light

When you flip on a light switch, electricity flows through to the light bulb. It passes through a small wire inside the bulb, then it heats up and glows bright. This produces the light that helps us see.

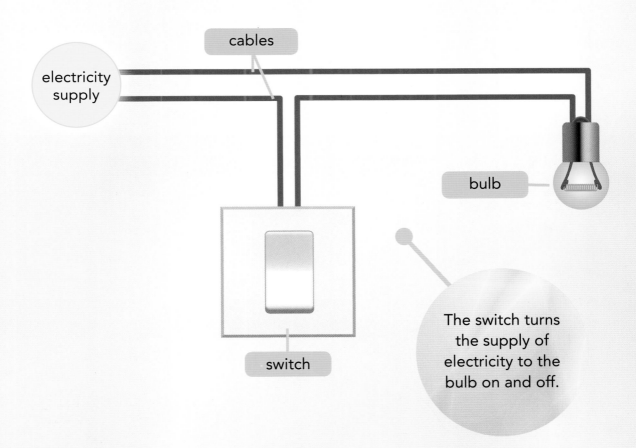

cables

electricity supply

bulb

switch

The switch turns the supply of electricity to the bulb on and off.

Water for Homes

It's easy to get water at home. You just turn on the faucet and out it comes! But where does the water come from, and why does it come out when you turn on the faucet?

Water is stored in ponds and lakes called **reservoirs**. Powerful pumps push the water along pipes from the reservoirs to homes. The pumps make a push called water pressure. This pushes the water out of faucets. You can feel the push if you block the flow of water.

This reservoir supplies homes with water.

reservoir   pond or lake where water is stored

Water and gravity

Some faucets in your house might be connected to a water tank high up in your home. **Gravity** pulls the water down from the tank, making it come out of your faucets.

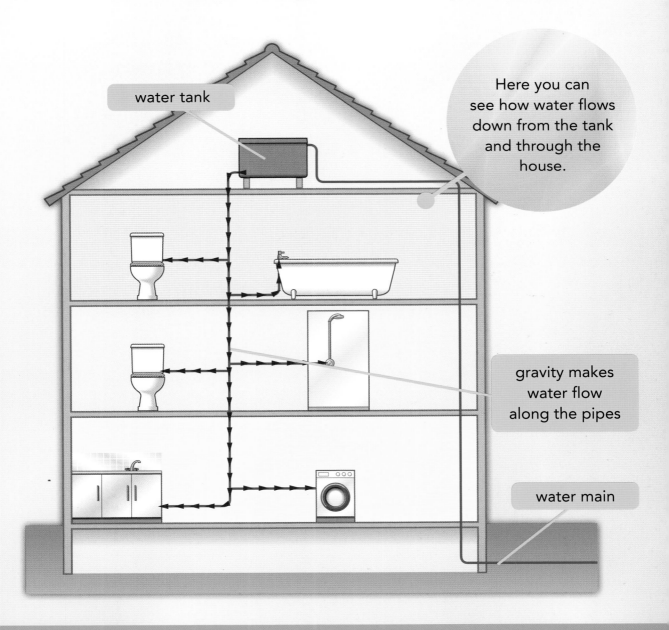

water tank

Here you can see how water flows down from the tank and through the house.

gravity makes water flow along the pipes

water main

gravity force that pulls things down to the ground

Down the drain

When you wash the shampoo from your hair in the shower, where does the water go? All the dirty water from your shower, your bath, your toilet, your kitchen sink, and your washing machine flows into pipes under the ground. The pipes are called drains. These pipes slope gently downhill. Gravity makes the water flow along them and into larger pipes, called sewers.

Measure up!

In the United States, a person uses about 100 gallons (378 liters) of water every day at home. Can you figure out how much water is used in your home every year? You need to follow this formula:

Water used each year in gallons (liters) = 100 (378) x number of people in the home x 365 days in the year.

Where does the dirty water from your home go?

Cleaning dirty water

Dirty water flows along sewers to a **sewage treatment plant**. Here, the water is cleaned. First, waste and grit are removed from the water. Then, it is cleaned by **microbes**. They eat any harmful germs in the water. The clean water flows into rivers or the sea.

This is a sewage treatment plant. The round beds that you can see contain the microbes that clean the water.

sewage treatment plant   place where dirty water from homes is cleaned
microbe   living thing that is too small to see

19

Machines That Help Us

Look around your kitchen at home. What tools can you see that you use for preparing food? You might find scissors, can openers, bottle openers, and nut crackers. All these tools are for cutting, opening, and squeezing things. They help us do jobs that we could not do with our hands. They make the jobs easier for us.

All these tools are simple machines that help with jobs in the kitchen.

Using levers

These tools are all made from **levers**. A lever is a rod that is fixed in one place, called a **pivot**. We use levers to cut and squeeze things. Levers make push and pull forces bigger.

We also use simple tools in the yard, such as shears and spades. We use tools such as pliers, screwdrivers, and hammers for do-it-yourself jobs.

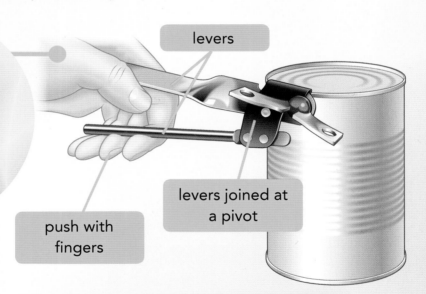

A can opener uses levers to work. Pressing the handles together makes the cutting wheel slice into the can.

levers

levers joined at a pivot

push with fingers

Stay safe
Levers can make very big forces. You should always be very careful with kitchen tools, because they can cut or crush your fingers. Never play with these kinds of tools.

lever   rod that is fixed at one point
pivot   fixed point at which a lever turns

Appliances

Does your home have a refrigerator, a washing machine, or a dishwasher? These machines are called **appliances**. Appliances make life easier for us. They do jobs for us and save us time. Other appliances include ovens, freezers, toasters, and microwaves.

Each time you fill up a dishwasher, you must put in some detergent.

Help with cleaning

A dishwasher washes dirty plates, cups, and silverware. It needs a supply of **electricity** and water. It also needs **detergent**. Detergent is a cleaning material that attracts grease and dirt. It pulls it off the things that are being cleaned. The water washes the grease and dirt away. Electricity works the moving parts of the dishwasher and heats the water to make it hot. A washing machine washes clothes in the same way.

appliance machine, such as a dishwasher, that is used in the home
detergent cleaning material that gets dirt and grease off dishes or clothes

Measure up!

Appliances are tested to see how much electricity they need to work. Appliances that use less electricity than others are better. They do not waste as much energy. Saving energy is good for our planet.

When a dishwasher has finished washing, all the dirt and grease from the dishes has gone down the drain.

Science in Your Life

Did you realize that there was so much science going on in your home? Science explains why builders choose different materials for building homes, and how we keep our homes warm or cool. Science explains why water comes out of our faucets, and how dirty water is cleaned. It explains how lights and machines in our homes work.

Saving energy

Most **electricity** is made at electricity-generating stations. Coal, oil, and gas are burned at these stations to make the electricity. We also burn them in some central-heating systems. Burning these **fuels** is harming our planet. So we should try to use less energy at home.

We should **insulate** our homes properly to stop heat from escaping when it is cold. We should also use **appliances** that use as little electricity as possible. We should switch things off when we are not using them. That way, we can help our planet.

insulate   prevent loss of heat

Stay safe

Fires sometimes start by accident in homes. Smoke alarms detect smoke from fires. They warn people that a fire has started. Smoke alarms are put on ceilings or high up on walls because smoke always rises upward. This is an example of how science in the home can help to save lives.

This man is installing a smoke alarm in a home.

Try It Yourself

Make a solar collector

In hot areas of the world, the sunshine has lots of heat energy in it. The energy is called **solar energy**. We can use this energy to heat water for washing and cleaning in homes. We catch the energy with a solar collector.

You can make a simple solar collector to see how it collects the energy in sunshine. You need a sunny day to do this experiment.

What you need:

- two small plastic water bottles (the same size)
- black poster paint
- a paint brush
- aluminum foil

What to do:

1. Take any labels off the bottles. Make sure the bottles are clean and dry.

2. Paint one of the bottles with black poster paint. Let the paint dry completely. You might need two coats of paint to cover the bottle completely with paint.

3. Wrap the second bottle in aluminum foil.

4. Fill both bottles with cold water. Be careful not to get water on the black paint.

5. Stand the bottles in the sunshine and leave them for about an hour.

6. Pour some water out of each bottle onto your hand. Which water is the warmest?

The black bottle collects solar energy, which makes the water inside warm. Sunshine bounces off the bottle covered with foil, so the water inside stays cool.

bottle painted black

bottle covered with aluminum foil

Glossary

appliance machine, such as a dishwasher, that is used in the home

boiler machine that burns fuel to heat water

cement gray powder that turns hard when it gets wet

concrete very hard building material, similar to rock

detergent cleaning material that gets dirt and grease off dishes or clothes

electricity form of energy used to make light and heat, and to power machines

element wires that heat up when electricity flows through them

forced-air heating heating system that spreads warm air through ducts and vents

foundation part of a home that stops it from sinking into the ground

frame pieces of concrete and metal joined together that hold up a building

fuel material we burn to make heat or power, such as gas, oil, or coal

gravity force that pulls things down to the ground

insulate prevent loss of heat

insulation material that stops heat from leaking out of a home

lever rod that is fixed at one point

microbe living thing that is too small to see

mortar solid material made from cement and sand

pivot fixed point at which a lever turns

property what a material is like (such as how hard it is)

reservoir pond or lake where water is stored

sewage treatment plant place where dirty water from homes is cleaned

socket place where you can plug in an electric machine

solar energy form of energy that is made by the Sun and that can be used to make electricity

structure strong shape that holds up a building

temperature how hot or cold something is

texture how a material feels (whether it is rough or smooth)

Find Out More

Use these resources to find more fun and useful information about the science behind homes.

Books

Deboo, Ana. *Safety Around the House* (*Tough Topics*). Chicago: Heinemann Library, 2008.

Ganeri, Anita, and Chris Oxlade. *Down the Drain: Conserving Water* (*You Can Save the Planet*). Chicago: Heinemann Library, 2005.

Haslam, Andrew, David Glover, and Jon Barnes. *Building* (*Make It Work!*). Chicago: World Book, 2008.

Spilsbury, Richard and Louise. *In the Home* (*Technology at Work*). Chicago: Raintree, 2008.

Wheeler, Jill C. *Everyday Conservation* (*Eye on Energy*). Edina, Minn.: ABDO, 2008.

Websites

www.eia.gov/kids/energy.cfm?page=3
Visit this website to find out all the ways we use electricity, from our homes and offices to transportation and more.

www.metrocouncil.org/environment/Kids/01.htm
Learn about waste water treatment and why it is important for animals and the environment.

www.energystar.gov/index.cfm?c=kids.kids_index
Find out lots of ways to help the environment by saving energy.

www.pbs.org/wgbh/buildingbig/
Learn more about how buildings are constructed. This website offers lots of interesting facts and some interactive features.

Index